HOW TO DEAL WITH DIFFICULT PEOPLE

Powerful Tactics for Dealing With Difficult People

(Expert Tactics for Dealing With Difficult People)

Janet Schorr

Published by Sharon Lohan

© **Janet Schorr**

All Rights Reserved

How to Deal With Difficult People: Powerful Tactics for Dealing With Difficult People (Expert Tactics for Dealing With Difficult People)

ISBN 978-1-990334-74-0

All rights reserved. No part of this guide may be reproduced in any form without permission in writing from the publisher except in the case of brief quotations embodied in critical articles or reviews.

Legal & Disclaimer

The information contained in this book is not designed to replace or take the place of any form of medicine or professional medical advice. The information in this book has been provided for educational and entertainment purposes only.

The information contained in this book has been compiled from sources deemed reliable, and it is accurate to the best of the Author's knowledge; however, the Author cannot guarantee its accuracy and validity and cannot be held liable for any errors or omissions. Changes are periodically made to this book. You must consult your doctor or get professional medical advice before using any of the suggested remedies, techniques, or information in this book.

Upon using the information contained in this book, you agree to hold harmless the Author from and against any damages, costs, and expenses, including any legal fees potentially resulting from the application of any of the information provided by this guide. This disclaimer applies to any damages or injury caused by the use and application, whether directly or indirectly, of any advice or information presented, whether for breach of contract, tort, negligence, personal injury, criminal intent, or under any other cause of action.

You agree to accept all risks of using the information presented inside this book. You need to consult a professional medical practitioner in order to ensure you are both able and healthy enough to participate in this program.

Table of Contents

INTRODUCTION 1

CHAPTER 1: NON-CONFRONTATIONAL STRATEGIES FOR DEALING WITH DIFFICULT PEOPLE AT WORK 4

CHAPTER 2: THE NON-DEFENSIVE ART OF LISTENING 15

CHAPTER 3: HOW TO DEAL WITH DIFFICULT PEOPLE AT WORK 20

CHAPTER 4: MINIMIZING INTERACTIONS WITH REALLY DIFFICULT (IMPOSSIBLE) PEOPLE 27

CHAPTER 5: MAKING TMDS - TOUGH MANAGEMENT DECISIONS 56

CHAPTER 6: THE ANGER ADDICT 64

CHAPTER 7: HOW TO DEAL WITH DIFFICULT PEOPLE IN PUBLIC 72

CHAPTER 8: CONFRONT THE DIFFICULT PERSON AND USE "I" STATEMENTS 76

CHAPTER 9: EFFECTIVE ATTITUDE 81

CHAPTER 10: DEALING WITH OFFICE OR WORK RELATIONSHIPS 109

CHAPTER 11: HOW TO DEAL WITH A DIFFICULT BOSS AND STILL KEEP YOUR JOB 115

CHAPTER 12: GETTING OUT OF TIGHT SITUATIONS 119

CONCLUSION 145

Introduction

You probably have dealt with difficult people ample times throughout your life. Difficult people are inevitable. Unfortunately, this inevitability is very hurtful. Nothing can ruin your day like a difficult person. Difficult people are able to make you doubt yourself and your efforts, while presenting you with intense hurdles that you must jump over.

You probably deal with difficult people in your work, your family, and even your social group. Whether you deal with a difficult boss or customers every day at work or you deal with people who hurt you in your family, you are probably bombarded with people who seem to be out to get you. These people say hurtful things to you, or they refuse to work with you. You find life to be more challenging because of their influences.

Don't let difficult people ruin your day. Difficult people usually have personal problems that they take out on you. It is not your problem that they are so hard to get along with and that they are so unpleasant to be around. Sadly, you may take many people too seriously. It is time to remove the seriousness from difficult situations so that you can enjoy your life.

You also need to learn how to move past difficult people. It is possible to work around difficult naysayers in your life and get your way. It is also possible to persuade difficult people to get along with you and work with you better. There are many ways that you can undermine the difficulties that difficult people create in your life.

It is possible to find ways to work with difficult people more easily. It is also possible to condition yourself to stop taking difficult people so personally. This book offers you ample tips on how to minimize the damage that these difficult people cause you.

Chapter 1: Non-confrontational Strategies for Dealing with Difficult People at Work

Difficult people exist everywhere, even in the workplace. Not only can the presence of such people make work seem less enjoyable, they are also capable of thwarting your career progress. Your capability to handle difficult people depends on three things:

Your level of self-esteem

Your level of self-confidence

Your professional courage

You might ask yourself "why is there a need to handle them?" Can you not just ignore them and continue with your work? Well, the thing about difficult people is that when the issues are left unaddressed, they tend to worsen. Ignoring the conflict will not cause the tension to disappear. Rather, it will simply simmer below the surface, creating counterproductive vibes. This is not something that you'd want to live with in the long run, not when it affects your livelihood and the satisfaction that you derive from your career.

When someone treats you in an unprofessional manner, you may feel shocked and hurt. Leaving the conflict unresolved for long periods may cause you to snap eventually. By addressing the issue as soon as possible, you are able to handle it in a calm and objective approach. Instead of finding solutions regarding the difficult co-worker, some people simply content themselves with complaining. The danger in this is that you'll end up earning the reputation of a whiner. Managers will come to see you as someone who is incapable of finding solutions to your own problems.

In the worst-case setting, your inability to deal with problematic co-workers will cause the others to label you as a difficult person as well. This is a kind of sticky tag that is hard to shake off and can thus ruin not just your image but your career as well. Furthermore, if the matter continues to go unsettled and met with nothing but constant complaints, your manager might end up deciding that you are a high maintenance employee and should therefore get replaced by someone who is more professional and someone who is capable of cooperating with coworkers. This isn't good particularly in the current job market where there are a lot of proficient workers getting laid off.

So what should you do then? Should you leave a can of foot powder for a colleague with smelly feet? Should you place a cockroach inside your boss's drawer? Should you combat your coworker by encouraging the others to gang up on him? All of these approaches seem juvenile and are more likely to get you fired. Do you feel yourself dreading going to work just to avoid one particularly problematic person? Do you feel like you should do something, but lack the courage to face your difficult workmate? If so, then you might want to start with a non-confrontational approach.

☐ Examine yourself.

Sometimes, the courage you need is not to confront a colleague, but to admit that you're wrong. The first thing to do would be to determine whether you're the only one who's affected by the difficult coworker's attitude. If others at work are able to perceive the same person as a difficult person, then chances are it isn't your fault. Perform an honest assessment of yourself. Ask yourself: Is the problem partially created by myself? Is there anything that I can do to improve the situation?

☐ Shield yourself.

While you may be itching to get even, stop. Establish boundaries for yourself. Be careful about what you say and who you say it to. While the urge to backstab and gain some sympathy may seem irresistible at some point, you might end up saying things that you will regret later on. If you **must** talk about the problematic person with someone, then choose to confide in individuals who are trustworthy and not just anyone who's willing to lend an ear. As much as possible, you should refrain from talking about the problem to people who know nothing of it and have nothing to do with it. Try not to involve anyone who cannot help in providing positive solutions for the problem. While you might think that recruiting peers to build a support system for yourself is a good idea, remember that your topmost priority should be to retain the respect of your colleagues.

☐ Understand your reaction.

Determining your own reaction to the difficult person's behavior can provide you with an idea as to what his motivation is. Has he succeeded in playing you? Are you giving him exactly what he wants?

Assess your feelings. Know whether your coworker's actions make you feel degraded, undermined, or manipulated. Do you end up having outbursts that you later on regret? Do you end up saying "yes" when what you should really say is "no"? Is your voice being stifled and is this preventing you from sharing your brilliant ideas in business meetings?

After an honest evaluation, decide whether your reaction is in proportion to the situation or whether you are just overreacting.

☐ Determine the motivation.

Why are they doing this? To solve your problem with a difficult coworker, you should first find out what his motivations are. Find out if there is a reason why he's displaying this negative behavior and discover what this reason is. Difficult coworkers are normally divided into two categories. These are the people who seek attention and those who avoid attention.

The Know-it-all

These people tend to act superior and are often sarcastic. They make themselves feel good by making you feel incompetent. They speak to you in a condescending tone and may display intimidating behavior.

The Bully

These people are aggressive and sometimes even hostile. They are loud and influential, and they might even abuse you.

The Complainer

These people moan loudly about their problems. They have a tendency to siphon your strength and to waste a great deal of your time with their complaints. Sometimes, they expect you to fix **their** problems.

The Silent Type

These include co-workers who are almost impossible to engage in conversation. You have a hard time gaining their participation.

The Yes Person

These co-workers have a tendency to say yes to everything. They seem to agree to just about anything. They may seem great at first until you realize that they are incapable of fulfilling their promises.

The Negativist

These pessimists whine about everything. They have a tendency to ruin the general vibe of the workplace as their negative thoughts often turn out to be contagious.

The Indecisive Worker

These people are incapable of making their own decisions. They keep waiting for you to initiate things. Their dependency can grow toxic overtime.

Notice that all of the personality types listed above display selfish behaviors. Each of them are simply trying to get what they want and often at your expense. Now how do you deal with them?

Observe closely and you'll realize that the last four types of people in the list display attention-avoiding behaviors. These people often benefit from support, encouragement, and inspiration.

Meanwhile, the first three types of people on the list manifest attention-seeking behaviors. You can solve this problem in a non-confrontational manner by refusing to gratify their behavior. The more you keep feeding them with attention, the more you are encouraging their difficult behavior. Here's what you can do to maintain peace and avoid conflict:

Minimize your time of being in the same room together.

Try not to directly communicate with the individual.

Make it extra difficult for them to reach you.

When an email from this person is unimportant or have absolutely nothing to do with work, either you ignore it or delegate it to someone else.

Now, that doesn't seem very courageous does it? Perhaps. But it prevents unnecessary struggles and allows you to maintain a modicum of civility. But what if these subtle strategies fail to work? Find out what you can do in the following chapters.

Chapter 2: The Non-Defensive Art Of Listening

Respect can be cultivated through giving. When you give respect, you shall definitely receive respect in return.

Respecting someone else's point of view is the respect most people lack. In this case you are required to learn to respect people's body language, their opinions and how they see things, without the need to condemn or even make them feel like they are not capable.

Do not judge or show the sign of discomfort when someone is making an effort to express themselves. Your tone and body language should agree with you.

Decide to approve them and to accept their opinions on the basis of respect, not on the basis of passivity.

The art of active listening is very important in achieving such effectiveness.

Firstly, you need to understand exactly the purpose for your active listening exercise. Keep these points in mind in order to stay motivated and focused while pursuing betterment in the communication world.

You listen to learn

You listen to enjoy what people are saying

You listen to actually understand people

You listen to obtain information from people

Respond by not responding

Sometimes the best way to listen to people is to not respond to them. You need to be so attentive, or fake attentiveness until you're actually attentive.

Only respond when they need you to respond. Do not respond by attacking the speaker or condemning what they just said.

Respond appropriately

The appropriate kind of response is not always agreement. Firstly, you need to make it clear that you respect their opinions.

In fact, you should applaud them for making an effort to actually say those things loud, then you can voice your concerns. It doesn't have to be a disagreement, just show your concerns.

Defer judgment

Stay away from being judgmental. People are too sensitive to judgment, it discourages them and make them feel frustrated.

Since amongst the purposes of listening is building perspective towards new information, focus on the information at hand and refrain from active judgment.

You need to allow them to finish by not interrupting with counter arguments.

Focus on the feedback system

Different people hear things differently. In order to be clear about what you are hearing, it is good to ask questions and to require a kind of explanation about a confusing subject matter.

Paraphrasing is one of the best ways people achieve such.

Show that you are listening

Faking it until you make it, you need to boost the other person's confidence by actually showing that you are listening.

Encourage the person with small verbal comments such as huh, yes, etc. Make sure your posture is aligned to the person, open and inviting.

Facial expressions relevant to the situation and nodding occasionally, will make you look like the great listener.

Actually pay attention

People want your attention, and they may decide to frustrate you until they get the attention.

Some ways of actually paying attention is by listening to the person's body language, avoiding side conversations, being mentally inclined with the subject matter, putting aside distracting thoughts and ultimately looking at the speaker directly.

Chapter 3: How To Deal With Difficult People At Work

The work place can be a very dramatic place. The combination of an ill-tempered customer, whinny colleagues, and a cranky boss can be sometimes too much to handle. It is likely that you have experienced irritating behaviors from your colleague or your boss that may have upset or stressed.

The tips below will help you deal with difficult people in your workplace:

1. Keep in mind your workmates are human

You have to accept the fact that everybody has a bad day sometime. This happens to the best of us and nothing you can do can change that. The only thing you can do is learn how to deal with these unavoidable circumstances.

Patience is sometimes the only thing you need when it comes to dealing with a moody colleague. Being patient to their negativity can help them realize when they are blowing things out of proportion. You can also show concern by asking if they are OK instead of overreacting. This normally neutralizes the difficulty in them and makes them see you as a supportive friend. This changes their bad attitude since the person now sees you as an ally and not an enemy.

2. Be tolerant of different personalities

Different people have different personalities. Your workplace is no different. It is very normal to work with people who approach and see things differently. Good examples of different personalities include the "do-er" type of people who are intolerant to discussions and only want to get things started, the other type is the know it all people who are always on top of everything, and the pessimists who are always pointing out the faults in almost every plan.

The above personalities may clash with you. This does not mean people with different personalities are dysfunctional; they are different. You should rectify your approach towards those with a personality different from yours by being observant. See how they approach issues. How their approach is different from yours. Then alter your style when communicating with them. For example if you have a-know-it all colleague who hardly considers any ideas, approach him or her with a plan full of factual details. This will help convince him or her since he or she believes in facts.

3. Manage expectations

Difficulty at work may come in the form of your boss assigning you urgent work some minutes before clock out, your colleague expecting you to answer a work email in the middle of the night, or a customer giving you difficult demands. These are all cases of misguided expectations.

To solve this kind of difficulties, sit down with your workmates and tell them what they should expect from you. For example, tell your boss to be giving you urgent work at a realistic period. When you have these conversations ahead of time, they will diffuse the difficult moments.

4. Be upfront

You can also deal with a difficult colleague by being upfront with the said colleague. Your workmates may not be self-aware of their abusive remarks or annoying behavior; therefore, it is incumbent upon you to inform these workmates of their wrongdoings. For example, if a colleague makes hurtful remarks towards you, you can pull him or her aside and ask why he or she is doing that. That person may be apologetic if he or she did not realize they were hurting you, or may accuse you of doing the same. Either way, you will have informed them and they will know it is not acceptable to do that.

5. Be considerate of psychological health issues

According to statistics, one in every four people experience mental health problem every year. When a colleague continually displays problematic and inappropriate behavior, the issue may lie deeper than happenings at the work place. There might be a psychological issue at play and you need to bear this in mind.

You can deal with this type of colleague by keeping your cool and using logic when you are around them. You can also politely pull your psychologically handicapped colleague to the side and have a hearty and supportive conversation about what is happening. This act will show them that you care, an action that can greatly reduce the person's destructive behavior towards you.

6. Assertively handle aggressive situations

If you have an overly aggressive colleague who verbally or physically abuses you, it is acceptable to walk away from that situation. It does not matter whether he or she is your boss or a subordinate staff. No one has the right to endanger your safety and wellbeing through psychological or physical fear in you. While this is on the extreme side of things, when you face a moderately aggressive workmate, you should maintain an assertive attitude towards the aggression. For example, when a difficult person is shouting at you, you can keep your voice cool or maintain a polite conversation when the person becomes rude. By doing this, you will show the person that he or she is overreacting, which will reduce his/her aggression.

7. Seek alternative methods

When you have tried using all the above methods and they have failed, you can opt for some last resort solutions that include avoiding crossing paths with a difficult workmate whenever you can, or you can file a formal complaint about their abusive behavior

Chapter 4: Minimizing Interactions With Really Difficult (Impossible) People

You have realized that no matter what you do, these people are not going to change. The only thing you can do is to minimize your interactions with them, if you can't cut them off. To keep your own sanity you need to learn how to navigate around these people. The constant demanding and difficult situations they create can sap your energy and make you miserable if you are not careful.

Stage 1: Acceptance

Learn to accept that this person will never become the type of person you want them to be. A good friend, an amiable colleague, an excellent boss is something you can never make out of them.

Inexplicable Compatibility Issues

When the issue seems to be only between you and them, it will be really hard to understand why the issue exists. The person may seem to get along with everyone except you.

Just accept that your personality types are such that you don't mesh well together. It is possible that there is nothing wrong with either of you, but you just bring out the worst in each other. There are many such relationships in the world.

A good relationship takes equal effort from both the people involved. You know you have done your best. Just let it be and concede that you both simply can't get along. It might as well be a huge difference in your core values. There is no reason to doubt yourself because you bring out the worst in each other.

The person might try to shift the blame onto you with a statement that everyone except, you likes them. Remember that shifting the blame to you does not alter the fact that the problem exists between the two of you. It is irrelevant how he is with others. It does not change the fact that he still negative with you.

Preserve your self-esteem

Don't let their attitude and the situation affect you in a bad way. You may start to think, What if the issue is with you? Do your best to maintain a positive self-image. The person is already making thing uncomfortable and difficult when he is present. Don't let the issue create self doubt, or lower your self- esteem that you are unable to live with yourself. Maintaining a good self-image is difficult when someone is saying you are bad or stupid etc., Instead of listening to what they say, focus on the more positive people around you. Look to people who tell you that it is not your fault. Interact with people who value you and your worth. You need to realize is that a difficult person tries to hurt you, to make themselves feel better. You need to realize a few things inherently

The difficult person is the one with a problem, not you.

They will try to shift the blame to you and try to make it your fault.

You can accept your flaws and improve yourself, so it's not you that is the issue.

They will try to bring you down and seek to justify and validate their actions.

You don't need to do that, because you already know your own worth.

If their insults don't have any truth to them, you don't need to take the accusations to heart.

The moment you realize that you are not at fault, you will feel much calmer, and their mudslinging will have the least effect.

Talk to someone

If the situation is affecting you negatively, and you don't know what to do, talk to someone close to you. Vent your frustrations for a little time and them forget about them.

Your friends may understand your frustration better. Even if they don't, just talking about the issue will help to relieve your mind off the tension and burden that you feel.

Be careful who you vent your feelings with. If the situation is at work, it might not be the best idea to vent to a co-worker.

You could write down your thoughts in a journal or on an online community. Writing what you feel often helps you get clarity about what you are feeling and may help you calm down.

Stage 2: Self Preservation

When you have difficult people in your life, it becomes difficult to keep yourself positive and unaffected by the negativity surrounding you. The negative influence can chip away at even the most well balanced person and make them break. Self preservation is an important part of learning to live with impossible people.

A reasonable interaction May be impossible

Realize that this person may never have a civilized and reasonable conversation with you. The only way they will talk to you is by putting you down and walk all over you. So don't let that happen. Don't take the blamed for everything, because they will never thank you for it, neither will they change.

Listen to what they say, stay silent and walk away. Know that nothing that comes out of your mouth will ever go to their heads.

Don't let them corner you into an argument. Always make sure someone else is there to intercept, just so you can minimize arguments.

Avoid arguing with them

Disagreeing with impossible people will not get you anywhere. If you can find ways to be agreeable with them use those methods, if not walk away.

Arguing with an impossible person is like trying to argue with a lamp post. It is not going to make any difference in their opinions.

It will instead rile your emotions up and put you off for the rest of the day.

When they come looking for a fight let them win, agree with them about what was the truth.

For example, if they fight with you saying that you were rude, or you did not consider their opinion once. Agree with them and say, "Yes, I am sorry I treated you that way then. Do I still do that now?"

If you don't have a fault now, they will be left with no accusations to swing at you.

Stay calm and detached from the interactions

Self preservation is the most important thing in your interaction with the impossible person. You know nothing you do can change that person.

Crying or getting angry will only make them even more difficult and strengthen the justification of their behaviour.

Instead when you stay calm and rational for enough time, they might start doubting their own reactions.

Don't take reactions from an impossible person personally, because their reaction is more about their failing than it is about yours.

Look at the situation more objectively and remove yourself emotionally from it. Learn to treat the situation with calmness and don't let the person bait you to respond in a negative way.

Being emotionally involved and getting angry can make you say things you don't mean, or things that you would not have said otherwise. These things will come back to bite you in the ass later on. So, count sheep in your head, do whatever it takes to calm yourself down before opening your mouth.

He/she needs your negative reaction to fuel the argument. If that is not available, the fight quickly looses steam and dies down by itself. If he still feels the need to argue, that is his problem and not yours.

If possible distract and redirect the conversation to something more positive once he/she has quieted down. This will help you soften the impact of your non-reaction to their outburst and let them know that you hold no hard feelings against them.

Do not be judgmental about them, because you do not have that right. You know nothing about what is going on in their heads, why they behave the way they do and judging them will not make you feel any better. In fact it will only make you feel bad, hopeless and helpless.

Ignore if possible

These people want attention. If they don't find what they want with you, they might move onto someone else. So if you can, ignore them as much as possible. Unless they cause issues that are disruptive or threatening do your best to avoid them. The more attention they receive from you, the more they are going to try to make you miserable, or disrupt your life

Don't let them into your head

You may not be able to avoid them in real life, but at least avoid letting them into your head. Even if you cannot avoid impossible people in your daily life, don't think about them on your "off" time. Remember that stressing about the person all the time is the same as giving him your precious time when he doesn't even care about you. Do other activities and make new friends; that way you aren't wasting time by thinking about what the person said or did constantly.

Confidence is Key

When you are dealing with a difficult person, the most important thing to remember is to stay confident in yourself and your opinion.

Stick to the facts and if you hold your ground, there is at least a chance that they might back down.

Being confident does not mean being rude, or cold or dismissive. Depending on the situation change the tone, but state your case with confidence.

Look them in the eye when you communicate. You do not want to be unsure when you communicate with them. If you are unsure, prepare yourself and make sure you can counter their reactions with reasonable answers.

But remember one thing; your ultimate aim is never to inflame or cause a fight but to send a message across.

Don't let them close

Difficult people very often try to use your personal information in any way they can to bring you down. So always take caution what you tell them. The most innocent comment can be taken and manipulated into an awful fabrication to paint you in a bad light.

This is the case especially, if the difficult person is good at manipulation. These people can be very good at getting you to tell them things about yourself.

Even when they act really friendly and kind they are generally fishing for things to pin on you or things that will bring you down. For example,

Your senior is a controlling perfectionist most of the time, and makes you anxious. Then some rare days she talks to you and tries to understand what your issue is. One day you confess that you are suffering from anxiety. A few days later you are asked to leave the job and take care of your health. The fact that your boss was responsible for your anxiety never came up.

So, telling the impossible person anything personal is probably not the best idea, and can sometimes have serious implications. Things you share with them in confidence can come back to haunt you out of the blue, be it your personal or professional life.

The difficult person may be an emotional abuser

These people are good at getting to the root of your insecurities. Their accusations and actions can humiliate and dominate. In some cases make you develop a negative trait aspect such as co-dependency. So what you can do when facing an emotionally abusive person is:

Don't let them affect your emotions

When you stop responding or reacting at first they might become even more angry

Eventually they calm down and stop because they realize that you will not be affected no matter what they do.

Then when they actually need your support, be kind.

Being kind does not mean you will let them cross a line, and they should be made aware of that right from the start.

Change the game

When you are suffering at the hands of difficult people, it's because they know your weaknesses. When you find yourself in situations where you can't escape then try to find ways to deal with them. Find out what will back them down, what are their triggers are. Just remember your aim is not to defeat that person or master them.

Consider the consequence of your every action towards them, it can be positive or it can be negative. Consider if you are ready to risk the situation to confront the person about their behaviour.

If you are too scared to act but are desperate for a change consider going to someone who you trust for help.

Ask for a reason

Sometimes asking the person what their issue is can be helpful. Just don't ask in an offensive way. For example,

"Why do you feel that I am not committed?"

"What is the reason for your anger?"

Show willingness to work with them to solve the issue.

There is a chance that the person may respond negatively to the fact that you are trying to solve the issue. In such cases it is best to let the issue go. There is a good chance that when you remain neutral, unaffected by the persons outburst that they may realize the issue lies with them.

So never react negatively to them as that only gives them fuel to continue behaving the way they are behaving. This is not to say, you let them walk all over you either.

Be prepared for unpredictable reactions

When difficult people start realizing that they are the ones who were difficult, there is usually an extreme reaction from them. Like a pendulum at the highest point when it is released. These people will quickly move from feeling like they are right to feeling like they are wrong about everything and back.

Their emotions will vary from one extreme to the other oscillating between the two emotions. They might just have an emotional meltdown.

This is a natural way of reacting, for anyone, when their strongly established reality is shattered. Everyone when their weakness is exposed has a hard time with it.

Don't let this surprise or confuse you, stay stable, positive and supportive but don't trust them too easily, because like the pendulum they are sure to oscillate between behaviours before finding their balance.

Boundaries

If the issue you have with the person relates to certain people, subjects, events etc., Make sure you tell them that if you are to continue interacting with them these subjects will not be discussed.

Set boundaries that should not be crossed, give them space and ask them to give you the space you need. State the rules about what is ok and what is not okay in the relationship.

If necessary write down your thoughts, organize them, get a clear picture of the problems you have with them. No matter how difficult it may seem, give them an ultimatum.

Make sure you focus on two things, the positives of not crossing boundaries, and the consequence of crossing them.

Make sure they have full power over their actions but not over yours.

Don't become like them

The tendency to adopt an emotion or trait whether positive or negative is something everyone has. If you find yourself behaving with the traits that you hate in the difficult person on accident, catch yourself from doing it.

If possible do your best to mimic the exact opposite trait, a positive to their negative. The more they try to get a rise out of you, the calmer you need to become. Tune them out, if you can't walk away.

Be the opposite of them

The best thing you can learn from an impossible person is how to be the one that is possible. You know what traits make them impossible to you. Implement the positives behaviours in your life, in contrast to their negatives. You may learn new things about people and about life from your situation that you can use positively in your life. A few things to realize,

You may not be able to keep them from being difficult that does not mean you should stop trying.

Like how bad behaviour from others can invoke the bad in us, consistently kind and good behaviour in spite of the others bad attitude might just shift their attitude and may influence the person for the better.

If you recognize you are not someone without faults, you will be able to accept others better. You may not be able to do the right thing every time, but try your best.

Be respectful and do the right thing, even if you do not receive anything in return. The issue with not behaving well is that it will catch up with them sooner or later in life; it is not your issue but theirs.

Realize that you will have both good and bad days, and if you slip up at some point take the courage to realize your mistakes and sincerely apologize for them.

Check your body language

How you stand, how you fold your hands, your facial expressions convey a lot to people. Non-verbal communication is a really important thing to take care of when we talk to the person. The body language reveals a lot of what you are feeling.

So take care to keep your posture more open and relaxed. Doing this consciously gives you an opportunity to relax and take better control of your emotions. Sometimes it helps to calm the other person down as well.

Take care to speak in a calm and certain way.

A steady and piercing stare should be avoided as this shows aggression.

Avoiding eye contact entirely is a sign of weakness.

Standing too close to the person and facing them directly is also a sign of aggression.

Focus on the positive

When you feel that you are losing control, remember that all people have redeeming traits, so try to think of something that is good about them. This might be something that the person is good at or a previous kindness or understanding they have been known to show.

If you can't think of anything that will make you think better of them then remember that everyone is imperfect and human, even you. Don't let yourself hate that person. It is unnecessary negativity that you don't need in your life.

You can learn and grow

When you deal with impossible people, often the worst of your nature comes out. You get to know about the flaws in your own character, your weaknesses and your strengths. You will learn to change yourself and grow from these experiences. You will learn to become a better communicator and gain a better understanding of human nature. These interactions will equip you with valuable and rich life lessons.

After this experience, you will be able to get along much better with other people. You may be younger than many, but your experiences will lend a new softness to your interactions with others. For example, here are a few things I leant from my experience at my previous job,

A good leader levels with a subordinate. In an office interaction, especially if you are not the boss but a peer. You need to be open and not act like you are the know-all authority in the team.

If you do, it will be sure to alienate the subordinate from you. They will not open up to you and tell you the reason for their issues, especially if the issues have to do with you.

Learn to take responsibility, when it is your fault. Don't be quick to blame your subordinates for an issue, which might have been caused by your inattention in the first place.

If you have a tendency to blame and berate a subordinate for issues/mistakes in the work that is meant to be handled as a team, it will cause insecurity amongst them.

This will make them try to undermine each other, as an act of self preservation.

You may initially ask what anyone would gain from hurting others needlessly. Now you understand that people would hurt others as a way to feel better or cope. The next time you encounter such situations, you will be able to keep a clear head and not react as you might have when you were less experienced. You will be able to handle difficult situations much better than you could before. The experience will lend you strength, flexibility and tolerance to gracefully handle the next difficult person that comes along.

End the relationship

If things do not change with the impossible person, after you have tried everything, it will be better to remove yourself from their vicinity. If they are a family member, it might be painful initially, but it might do both of you some good if you leave.

Keeping the relation up with an impossible person long term is not healthy.

If you feel like you are starting to lose yourself, it is a very good indication that you need to move out of that situation.

Even the most stable and positive person can get traumatised and develop negative effects eventually.

Do not go back to that person after that, ever, because after all the effort that you took and the chances that you gave the person has not changed. It should not be your problem if that person still continues to have issues with you.

You have one life to live and it is short. Find people who are more positive to surround yourself with.

If you can't leave due to some circumstances, then detach from them mentally and leave them as soon as you can.

It may seem painful and scary to leave, but afterwards once you find your way around and things will get better. You can move into a much better situation and be much happier.

If the issue is at a job, then consider transferring to a different team or part of the organization. Don't think you are acting out of cowardice; it is in fact a better option to choose if you know your health was getting affected in the company of the impossible person.

If that does not help then you can consider quitting your job, because no price is worth the risk of your happiness or sanity.

Stay if you think the good things are better than the bad or if it is the other way around.

Consider this information before you decide what you want to do.

Robert Waldinger, the present director of a 75 year long Harvard study, revealed the fact discovered in the study. The thing that makes humans live longer, healthier and happier lives is the good and healthy relationships they have in their lives. The study found that the one thing that influenced a long and prosperous life is not exercising or a job or money but good, strong and loving relationships.

So if not my word, take their experience into consideration. Life is short. With impossible people in it, it will be unhappy, unhealthy and much shorter. Don't be a martyr, be happy!

Chapter 5: Making Tmds - Tough Management Decisions

As a manager, there's no escaping one basic truth — you're paid to make the difficult decisions. You may or may not be paid well, granted, but that doesn't really matter; the title of 'manager' inevitably means that you'll have to make some tough solo decisions now and again. As the phrase goes, the buck stops with you.

You could be forced to make tough budget decisions, fire poor providers, stop certain product lines, scale back on investments or even reluctantly decide to let something go that isn't working. They're tough enough decisions to make. Yet, as we'll see in the second half of this book, these often tend to pale into insignificance when they compare to the decisions you may have to make about your personnel. These latter decisions may well be some of the most difficult problems you'll ever have to deal with in your career.

You may have to decide to change people's job descriptions, for instance, or cut their hours, choose which members of staff to make redundant or fire someone who just isn't working out... none of which will be easy decisions to make.

It's worth reiterating yet again that you are not in your job to get people to like you. That doesn't mean you have to be an ogre but as a manager your loyalty first and foremost is to the company. You are there to make money, not to be popular or to make friends with your staff. It's a bonus if they do like you but it's not essential to doing a good job. In fact, I'd say it's more important to be respected for making firm decisions than it is to be liked. After all, ask yourself: how would your employees treat you if they were the boss? Would they let you get away with things in a bid to be liked? Probably not!

A true leader can make the big decisions. There's a theory that says that 95% of the decisions a CEO makes can be made by any reasonably intelligent person who has graduated from secondary school, but those aren't the decisions that really matter. The CEO instead is getting paid to make the other 5% of decisions, the really hard ones. Those are the ones that not just anyone can do. You may not be a CEO just yet, but the same rule of thumb applies: how you handle that 5% marks out just what kind of boss you really are.

In my career, I've had to let people go several times. In a couple of cases it was due to redundancy; with others, it was a case of not extending their contract, while one was sacked for gross misconduct. I'd be lying if I told you I could remember all of their names; I can't. Not anymore. That doesn't mean that I didn't dwell on the decisions at the time though, or pore through the documentation looking for other options. Some had plainly deserved their fate; others were victims of circumstance while others still were let go for rather less obvious reasons.

The only ones that bother me now, so many years later, are the ones where I still wonder if I could or should have made a different choice. Ask any manager and they'll no doubt have the same concern. At the end of the day, however, I made the most objective decision I could make at the time with the information at hand. That's all you can do.

So, if you're faced with a difficult decision, just how can you make sure you can make the best and most objective decision for your company?

First, **trust your instincts**. Your gut should tell you what you really want to do, so make sure you listen to it.

Before you do anything, **understand the need for change**. Some decisions may be automatic, while others are caused by a change in circumstances. The worst kind of manager is one who refuses to act when needed; it fosters resentment from employees as well as poor business practices. Putting your head in the sand doesn't help anyone so start by recognising and respecting the need for a decision.

Make sure you **understand the problems**, opportunities or issues at play. Gather as much information about the situation or problem you face as possible; make sure you understand why you need to make the decision in question. Don't just gloss over it; an in-depth appreciation for the problem at hand will help to guide you to the appropriate response and course of action, not to mention allow you to anticipate potential problems that may arise in the future.

Assess the alternatives. Don't just fall back on creating one course of action; create many and test them out in your head. Assess the benefits and pitfalls of each. This not only gives you more than one option to choose from, but it may well help you personally with the decision in the future. If the decision you end up making impacts people's jobs and livelihoods negatively, for instance, you're going to want the peace of mind of knowing that you thought through and tried out every alternative before settling on your final choice. It's also the least that you owe your team.

While a manager's life can be solitary – it's lonely at the top, remember – you might want to **ask external professionals for advice** or insight into your problem or decision. Some towns and cities have professional groups where managers come together for support and mentoring.

Obviously, make sure you trust the person involved first.

When you've done all of that, **consider the most effective alternative**, taking into account all possible outcomes.

Always **do what you think is right** for your team, your business, your customers and the company as a whole. Keep that at the front of your mind; it makes the choices you have to make much more matter of fact.

Make the decisions with honour. If you have to make tough decisions about your team, don't use it as a reason to settle old scores or to deal with personal issues, favouritism or preferences. This is a business decision; don't dilute it with personalities. Step back from your thought process from time to time to assess if you are truly being objective. It's much easier to hold your head up high when you explain the changes to your team that way.

Avoid emotion. If you can eschew sentiment, you'll actually find the decision easier to make. Staying factual and objective should make the right choice obvious and clear-cut, if not painless.

Just because you've made the decision and now put it into action, doesn't mean you have to stop there. Make an effort to **learn from the outcome of your decision** – what worked and what didn't – and listen to any feedback. It will stand you in good stead for any future decisions that need to be made.

Chapter 6: The Anger Addict

It is quite easy to become agitated or disturbed when an angry person confronts you. You even run the risk of making the situation worse when you do not know how to properly react to the anger. It is only possible to stay in control of the situation when you learn how to react in a calm manner and with empathy. When you do so, you will be viewed as a courteous professional who knows how to deal with difficult situations.

Here are effective techniques to deal with people who use anger as their defense mechanism or as a means to get what they want.

Always make sure that you are safe

As much as possible, do not allow yourself to be alone with an angry person. Always involve other people. When you sense that the person you are talking to is starting to become threatening, you need to trust your instincts and leave the room instantly especially if you sense that your personal safety is at risk or if you think you have become too distressed to handle the situation properly. Seek assistance from your boss or from a colleague that you can trust. When appropriate, immediately report the incident to the angry person's superior or to the Human Resources Department.

Avoid responding with anger

It is but natural for us to become hurt when we are confronted by an angry person. This is true whether they have the right to be angry with us or not. When someone gets angry at us, we feel like we are being attacked and our body will get into its "fight or flight" mode which can result to us being angry too. But even with that natural instinct of becoming angry, you need to make the effort of responding in a calm and intelligent manner when confronted by an angry person. Practice deep breathing which can help you to remain calm even in the midst of tense situations. If you sense that your anger is starting to increase, courteously excuse yourself so you can calm yourself down.

Distance yourself from the situation emotionally

There are times when a person's anger seems to be directed at you when it really has nothing to do with you. When you are able to identify these instances, you can better deal with angry people because you will not get upset and retaliate. Some people are not able to vent their emotions to the right people or things and so they simply lash out atthe first person that they see. These people are actually using their fury to make themselves feel better. The best that you can do is to simply become emotionally distant when confronted by an angry person. Tell yourself that you are not involved in the other person's anger and you should stay uninvolved.

Help in identifying the cause of the anger

To help yourself in distancing yourself emotionally from the situation, you can help the other person in identifying the root cause of his anger. Persuade the angry person to think why he is feeling very angry, but make sure that you do not interrupt him while he is still speaking. Simply ask effective questions until he has completely explained his thoughts and emotions. As much as you can, try to view things from his perspective while he is making his explanations. Show him that you are really listening to what he is saying. When it is your turn to speak, make sure that your voice is calm and low. Do not speak fast and avoid using threatening body language. Allow your calm demeanor to influence the other person to calm down, as well.

Alsoavoid using general statements. Do not just say words like"Oh, that really sounds frustrating"or"I know how you feel". The other person might think that you are just saying those words without meaning them. What you can do is to paraphrase what the other person has said to let him know that you understand what he is saying. Show as much empathy as you can. Show him that you are willing to help him in looking for the solutions to the problem. You can also show your respect by not being judgmental of the other person's negative behaviors. Remind yourself that you can get angry too and you still want to be respected when you are angry.

Distract the angry person

You can neutralize the anger of a person by helping him focus his awareness on another thing. When you allow the other person to ponder or contemplate more on the reason why he is angry, it will only increase his angry feelings. However, when you distract him from his negative feelings, you can lessen the anger. You can use humor appropriately to lighten the mood or you can change the subject to something that you think he can be excited about, but rememberthat this technique is normally effective for people who are only tolerably angry. It doesn't normally work with people who are intensely angry because they may only get annoyed when they feel that you are not letting them vent out their emotions.

Help the other person control his anger

When a member of your team always bursts out inanger, the rest of your team can become affected. One person's anger can lower the morale and overall productivity of the entire group. This is why supervisors and managers should learn how to mentor or coach their subordinates so that they will learn how to better control their emotions.

Learn how to defuse anger

If your job role requires you to regularly cope with angry people, you should make sure that you are properly protected. Job roles that are emotionally demanding are not only tiring physically but emotionallyas well. You may notice that at the end of the day, you are drained of all your energies. You need to equip yourself with tools and skills that can help defuse other people's anger so that you will not have to absorb it all the time. You can work with your colleagues or teammates so you can practice how to deal with upset and angry customers. Other skills that you may need to develop include assertiveness, good communication skills, and emotional intelligence.

Learn how to communicate your own feelings

When you need to regularly work with someone who always has angry outbursts, it is not healthy to simply wait for his anger to pass every time. You need to learn how to communicate your own feelings to the other person so that he will understand how his anger affects you. But you should not use critical statements when you talk to the angry person. When you start your sentences with a "you", you may only trigger him to become defensive and angry. Do not blurt out: "You can really upset the whole group with your constant anger and screaming" because this will only make him angrier. You can still show respect even when you are being assertive. One way to do this is to start your sentences with an "I" to effectively communicate your own feelings. You can say, "I become upset and stressed out every time you scream and yell during team meetings. I find it more difficult to think of possible solutions when I am stressed out."

Chapter 7: How To Deal With Difficult People In Public

In complete contrast to people you deal with at home; you come across a lot of different personalities and characters in public and only for a brief period of time. There are no real relationships established between them. What makes it equally challenging thought is that though these moments are fleeting but because you are exposed to so many factors.

Try to ignore and keep your cool

Since you're exposed to them for only a short period of time, it is best to ignore them when you can. Extending a bit of patience for the people you encounter in public will help you avoid conflict and making a scene easily.

Can you just imagine if you confronted every person that annoyed you in public? It will be such a riot. Think about it this way too, what benefit will you get if you confront the person? If the pain is greater than the rewards, it would be best to just wait it out and let the situation pass. With the many similar decisions you will make each day, chances are, by the end of the week, you won't remember anymore the person who stepped on your new shoes on the train on Monday or the person who stole your cab on Tuesday.

These are circumstances that won't matter five years from now, so don't let fleeting moments consume you or affect you the entire day, when more important things will happen.

Don't make a fuss

When you realize how inconsequential those moments are, it will be easier for you not to make a big fuss out of it. You might argue that the principle of the thing is bigger than the actual circumstance. The quick answer to that is to choose your fights.

Instances like these don't have to blown out of proportion. Remember that there are much worthier causes in your life, more important people so reserve your energy for the things and people who matter.

Tell them your intentions nicely

When you absolutely have to, express your request in a nice way, no matter how infuriated or frustrated you are. People are more likely to listen and respond to people who are calm and not run over by their emotions.

The problem might be as simple as they didn't notice that they're already annoying you. Once you point in out to them, the situation will be easily remedied. Remember that like you, these people also have to bear with the crush of thousands of people every day.

Let them be – walk away if you can

If the circumstance allows, make the shift so that you are no longer affected by the situation. The solution might not be so hard – like transferring seats in the movie theater or shutting the world out through some music in your earphones. Don't let your environment affect you.

Choose to be the bigger person and go into your happy place. The world is what you would like it to be, so focus on the good things rather than dwelling on the things that annoy you.

Chapter 8: Confront The Difficult Person And Use "I" Statements

This has to be the hardest of all of the methods of dealing with difficult people. No one likes confrontation. When we think of confrontation, we often think of going up to someone and saying, "You are really a mean person, why are you so mean to me? I never did anything to you." That is not the kind of confrontation that we want to do with a difficult person—especially someone at work or our neighbors.

There are several different ways to confront the issue that you and the other person have. We will start with the family. An example of a conversation with someone you love is meeting with this person in a quiet place where others are not in earshot. Always start the conversation with something positive.

"Grandpa, you know I love you more than anything in the world, and I understand that you are very lonely without Grandma. And I know that your arthritis makes you hurt all over. "I feel" bad when you tell me that. Is there something I can do to help you so you are not so sad? Can I take you to the doctor to see if there is some kind of medicine or herbs that will help you to not be in so much pain? I don't like to see you in pain."

There is always something that you might be able to do to help him, but be sure to use "I" statements. It takes the accusation curve off of the words. It won't put the other person on the defensive. And the person may not realize that he/she is having that kind of effect on others.

Then we have the neighbors, this one is going to be a little more difficult to do. Usually the kind words and acts will help. But if not, then a little meeting can help to get the ball rolling. Take over a plate of cookies and invite yourself in by telling them that you would like to speak with them about something that is important to you.

Start with a positive comment such as, "Your yard is so nice, your flowers are beautiful to look at and they make our yard smell so good. Thank you for being a good neighbor. I would like to return the favor and be a good neighbor to you as well. Is there anything that I can do to make that happen? Are we too loud—do we bother you with the kid's trumpet practice? Please feel free to let me know if we are annoying you in any way. We want to be the best neighbors we can be. Can we help you in any way?" More than that, there are not many other things to say or do. You have put yourself out there. The ball is in his yard now!

Finally, we find ourselves back at work. We have tried the common thread; we have tried the kind words, the random acts of kindness. Now we have one more avenue to explore.

If your difficult person is your boss, and all of the kind things you have said or done have not made any difference in how your boss treats you, then you have a few alternatives. (1) You can go to your Human Resources Department and speak to the director—not the secretary. Share your experiences with the director and hope for the best, (2) If the boss's behavior is sexual harassment or emotional harassment, you can speak to an attorney (especially if you have spoken with H.R. and nothing has been accomplished), or (3) You can ask to be transferred to another department or you can start searching for another job. Confrontations seldom work when you try to talk to a supervisor who treats you badly.

And, finally, if the difficult person is a coworker that you have to work closely with every day, you will need to ask to speak with this person somewhere in private. Again, start the conversation on a positive note. "You are the best scheduler I have ever worked with. I appreciate how well you take care of my orders," then add the "I" statements. "I feel like I am bothering you when I bring work to your desk. I sometimes feel that you might be angry with me. Is there anything that I do that offends you? Is there a better way for me to approach you with questions or requests? Is there a better time for me to do this? I would like to help out in any way that I can to make our working relationship better. Do you have any ideas how I can do that?"

Using the "I" statements keeps the difficult person from being on the defensive. And let's face it, you are the only one out of the two of you who cares enough to try to work things out or make them better. What this does is brings the behavior to the attention of the other person without accusing him/her of being rude. But it does bring it to his/her attention. At this point, it is time to move on to the next step

Chapter 9: Effective Attitude

Avoiding the Drama

Before we had children, Penny and I were talking with a wise couple about the familiar scene of kids throwing grocery store temper tantrums. They explained how they handled this situation with their own children, and we logged their idea for future reference, determined to employ the strategy should we ever need it. A few years later, Penny was in the checkout line and our little girl began begging relentlessly for a piece of junk on a rack nearby. Penny leaned over and said, "Begging is not allowed, and if you ask for it one more time, we'll go home." As expected, she begged again. Penny quietly picked her up, left the cart, and walked out of the store with our girl screaming her head off, conveying to shoppers that a kidnapping was in progress. Penny calmly strapped her into the car seat, drove home, and no other discipline followed. On the next grocery store trip, the begging started again. But this time Penny leaned over and said, "Now, I've told you that begging is not allowed. Remember what happened the last time?" That did it. No more begging. Displeasure, yes; begging, no.

What we see is a drama staged and a drama avoided. Our little girl staged the drama hoping to play the role of **master,** to be in charge. But remember, dramas only succeed if others play their parts. Penny avoided participation by neither giving in nor displaying aggravation—two different forms of participating. Therefore, the drama strategy failed and was not attempted the next time around. As good drama critics, let's review this play and make some post-drama observations.

To handle this situation so well, Penny had to go against her grain. She was prone to get pulled into the power struggle, get upset, argue, threaten, or (worse yet) give in to keep the peace. She countered her natural reactions by opting, instead, for preplanned responses. **Drama avoidance requires planning.**

The strategy cost her something—she had to go back to the store and shop again. But we had previously determined that the cost of reinforcing this undesirable pattern was higher than the time and energy it cost her to reshop. **Drama avoidance may cost something.**

In this case, our plan succeeded on the first attempt, but Penny was prepared to repeat the strategy if needed until it did work. **Drama avoidance requires persistence.**

The outcome of our plan had a good effect, in this case for both parties. Penny got to shop with less aggravation. Our girl was forced to grow up just a little bit that day, developing better ways of handling herself. **Drama avoidance brings about growth.**

Again, unreasonable people are children in the bodies of adults. They stage dramas not unlike the one just discussed, which succeed only if others participate. Participation provides a stage on which the unreasonable person's drama is performed. How can we avoid becoming drama participants? By avoiding three enticements: button pushes, reactions, and pushing buttons.

Avoiding Button Pushes

Unreasonable People Know Our Buttons

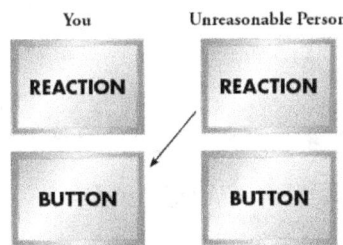

The unreasonable person pushes our buttons hoping for a reaction. He typically understands us better than we understand him. He or she knows where our buttons are and how to push them. Unreasonable people are good at enticing participation because drama success is perceived as necessary for their survival. Reasonable people are not naturally good at resisting enticements because that's not how we relate. Therefore, we must develop the skill.

Expect Attacks

The unreasonable person may push our buttons in predictably obvious ways or ambush us in unpredictably subtle ways.

Obvious Attacks

Examples of obvious attacks include insults, besmirching of character, slanderous accusations, name-calling, defamations, unjustified criticisms, and blatant lies. The unreasonable person taunts and eggs us on, hoping desperately for a knee-jerk reaction that places us squarely into the drama.

Subtle Attacks (Manipulations)

While obvious attacks are actively aggressive, subtle attacks are passively aggressive or manipulative. Our buttons get pushed, but we don't see the attacks coming. We get ambushed or sucker-punched. Let's look at four types of manipulations.

Exploitation of weaknesses. An invading army attacks at the weakest spot. Terrorists strike where their opponents are most vulnerable. Similarly, the unreasonable person sniffs out our weaknesses and attacks us there. We all have buttons—places of weakness, immaturity, and inadequacy. When life requires us to be strong in a weak area, an internal dialogue takes place. Some people use the word "tapes" to describe this self-talk, as in "When I took that job, all of my old inadequacy tapes started playing, telling me I couldn't do it." Others refer to the dialogue using terms such as "the voices," "the committee," or "the choir." One British writer described it using a phrase from wartime England: "the internal saboteur."[1] The unreasonable person, who wants to defeat us in conflict, studies our weaknesses and allies himself with our internal saboteurs. When certain buttons are pushed, the internal saboteurs spring into action, doing their best to remind us of our weakness and make us feel awful about ourselves. Like a voice-activated recorder, the sound of his voice on the outside activates the tapes on the inside. If we believe the tapes, we get sucked into the drama and the exploitation succeeds.

Suppose you are generous to a fault. You're a very giving person, but an old tape inside your head says, **You really could do more for people, you know. What's wrong with you? You're so selfish.** Suppose also that you have someone in your life like Patti's mom, a Level 2 martyr, whose stance is, "I can't make it without you to rescue me." She constantly demands assistance for problems she could easily fix herself. If you decline a request, she says, "That's fine. I'll do it myself. I thought you were here for me, but I guess I was wrong." Your internal saboteur springs into action saying, **She's right, you know. If you were a better**

person, you'd go out of your way to help her. What's wrong with you? You've been guilt tripped, and to escape the guilt, you acquiesce to the demand. Your weakness has been exploited, and you've become a player in the drama, saving a martyr supposedly in need of rescue.

Presumptions. Most of us have been taught to believe the best of people and to give them the benefit of the doubt. While reasonable people deserve such courtesies, unreasonable people don't. As a kind gesture, we may offer a ride to a hitchhiker. If he's a good guy, no problem. If he's a crook, our kindness gets us robbed. If we give an unreasonable person the benefit of the doubt, he may very well presume upon our good graces and use it to his advantage—a subtle attack.

Role shifts. If an unreasonable person can't entice us into playing the required part, he may shift roles in hopes that, when the drama ends, he'll be back in his preferred role.2 Here are some different forms of role shifting:

If the **master role** is preferred: A master needs us to submit. If we don't, he may shift into the **messiah role,** someone rescuing a person in need. He gives us something, but the gift has strings attached. At that point the giver is no longer a helper but a controller, the assistance being accompanied by an obligation to submit.

If the **messiah role** is preferred: A messiah is a sacrificial giver and needs us to be grateful recipients. If we aren't, she may slip into the **martyr role,** saying, "After all I've done for you, this is the kind of treatment I get? Thanks a lot." If it works, we'll allow her to resume the messiah role so we can escape the guilt trip discomfort.

If the **martyr role** is preferred: Martyrs are either saved by messiahs or persecuted by masters, the roles we must play for the martyr role to succeed. If we don't, she may become a **master** and strike at us, hoping we'll strike back. If we do strike back, she can once again assume the role of a martyr, a person who suffers at the hands of others: "I can't believe you would treat me this way."

If the **mute role** is preferred: A mute wants to be untroubled and needs us to pretend along with him that everything is just fine. If we refuse to participate in the pretense or enable the denial, he may assume the role of a **martyr:** "We could get on with our lives if you wouldn't keep bringing up all our problems. Can we please move on?"

These role requirements are button-pushing, boundary-violating drama enticements. There is pressure to perform our roles so that the other's role achieves the desired outcome—becoming the good guy. That's why it wears us out. We can't relax and just be ourselves.

Learn from Your Mistakes

Pickpockets can do their chosen profession because people aren't expecting their pockets to get picked. Remember, unreasonable people are good at enticements, but reasonable people are not naturally good at resisting enticements and can easily get caught off guard. We will make mistakes, and slip-ups are inevitable. But it's important to learn from our mistakes and avoid repeating them. Beating ourselves up about slip-ups doesn't help, but safeguarding ourselves against further enticements does. We should avoid situations in which mistakes are likely to happen and rehearse how to handle the situation should it happen again.

When Patti Avoided Button Pushes

Long before she came to see me, Patti used the term "subtly manipulative" to describe her mom. To casual observers, she was always the pleasant and productive Betty Crocker, but to Patti and Bill she was frequently a Bette Davis-type vixen. Patti learned she had to keep up her guard in this game of "emotional chess" between her family and "the vixen."

Patti's mom was quite adept at utilizing her arsenal of subtle weapons. Her daughter had a tender spot for people and animals in need and would go out of her way to provide assistance whenever she could. Understanding this, her mom would make her own needs apparent, taking on the demeanor of a wounded pet. These attempts to capitalize on Patti's bigheartedness usually worked. When they did, Patti felt angry and presumed upon one more time. Yes, her mom was manipulative, but Patti came to see that it was her responsibility to avoid manipulation. When she studied her own buttons and worked out a better response, it became much harder for her mom to push them.

Having to think this way about her mom left Patti with a bad taste in her mouth, reflected in statements such as, "I can't believe I have to be so guarded with my own mother. Isn't that terrible?" Actually, Patti wasn't being terrible, she was being wise. The guilt she felt for having negative feelings about her mom was unwarranted. Her bad feelings served a good purpose— to make her aware of boundary violations. She couldn't feel good about what her mother was doing, but she could make use of what she felt to move toward good conflict.

Avoid Reactions

Controlling your reaction when your button is pushed

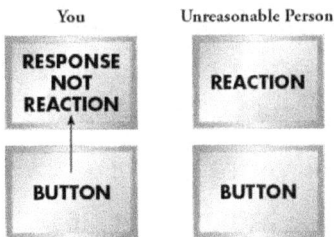

Rudyard Kipling must have known some cantankerous unreasonable people. He said, "If you can keep your head when all about you are losing theirs and blaming it on you..."[3] The unreasonable person desperately needs us to react, to lose our heads, so our reactions can be used as evidence that we're crazy and he or she is not.

Figuratively speaking, he takes "snapshots" of our reactions and uses those images to build the case—to himself and others—that we're bad and he's good. "Photo albums" displaying pictures of our bad behavior are eagerly shown around. Another way to think about this is that he has an emotional "remote control" for us. When he pushes our buttons and observes a reaction, he's gratified. But if he doesn't see a reaction, he's frustrated and will push the buttons more vigorously. To keep from reacting, we must plan our responses so we won't display any reaction, thus stopping the manipulation

Accepting the Limits

We've been discussing Patti, a person in conflict with an unreasonable person. Here's a similar story, only this conflict was not between individuals but between nations—the United States and the Soviet Union. In 1917, the Bolshevik Revolution occurred. The Russian monarchy was overthrown and replaced by a communist form of government. The new Union of Soviet Socialist Republics was founded upon Marxist principles, bringing radical changes to this vast country that stretched from Europe's border to the Pacific. Though allied against Hitler's Germany in

World War II, the United States and the Soviet Union distrusted each other, with suspicions coming to a head in the years following the war. The development of Soviet nuclear capabilities in the late 1940s kept tensions escalated for the next several decades as the planet endured the ever-present potential of thermonuclear annihilation.

We've all struggled to handle conflicts with individual unreasonable people. But in many respects, the United States at this time had to contend with a giant, global unreasonable person in the form of the Soviet Union. This applied not so much to individual citizens but to the communist leadership controlling the apparatus of government.

First, they had unused "reason muscles." Their worldview and ideologically driven commitments led them to believe:

The wrongness must be on the side of the U.S.

We only see where we're right.

If we're wrong, so what?

We're only bothered if the wrongness of the U.S. hurts us.

We're not wrong, so there is nothing to correct.

They truly believed they were good and the U.S. was bad. They accused the U.S. of the very things that were true of them. So great was their commitment to rightness that they were willing to sacrifice truth to maintain it. The ends justified the means. They believed that lying or any other vice was a virtue if it advanced the cause of world communism.

Second, they were Level 3 (dangerous) unreasonable people. They responded to conflict by threatening to annihilate the U.S. or anyone who challenged them.

Third, they were **masters** who needed others to play a subservient role. Their "satellites" in Eastern Europe had no independence, and any moves toward self-determination were soundly squelched by military force.

Fourth, Western nations, particularly the United States, experienced the same effects as those produced by individual unreasonable people. The USSR government drove us crazy, made us sick, and wore us out. The situation drained huge portions of our national resources.

Bad conflict is what happens when we react to each other's reactions. Armed with atomic weapons that could be delivered atop intercontinental ballistic missiles (ICBMs), the two nations could ill-afford bad conflict reactions. One of these almost occurred in 1962 when the Soviets attempted to deploy offensive nuclear weapons on the island of Cuba, placing American population centers within striking distance of Soviet missiles. This was unacceptable to the U.S. and, for a few days, the world teetered on the precipice of nuclear war, in which an attack by either side would have led to retaliation by the other. In this case, the reactive cycle would have resulted in millions of deaths.

To avoid the horrific effects of bad conflict, the two nations became engaged in what was called the "Cold War," a conflict in which few shots were fired but tensions remained escalated. It wasn't a hot, shooting war due largely to the policy of "Mutually Assured Destruction" (MAD). That is, a nuclear first strike by either side would trigger a retaliatory response by the other, assuring the destruction of the initiator. Thus, the policy served to deter first strike impulses. "Peaceful coexistence" was the term used to describe the Cold War relationship of the two superpowers. While MAD helped to lower the potential of bad conflict, there was still the question about how to have good conflict with a giant, global unreasonable person. A vigorous debate developed among Westerners about how peace could best be achieved.

Generally there were two schools of thought. The first was the "peace through reason" approach. This view held that the Soviet leaders were reasonable people and wanted peace just like us; we simply misunderstood each other. The expectation, therefore, was that Western disarmament gestures would impress the Soviets and be reciprocated by their own disarmament gestures, making the world an increasingly safer place. The other school of thought was the "peace through strength" approach. This view held that the Soviet leaders were less interested in peace and more interested in winning, in achieving their global ideological objectives. Consequently, Western disarmament gestures would simply be exploited by the Soviets, giving them a position of nuclear superiority and making the world an even more dangerous place.

For many years the "peace through reason" approach was attempted, and the Soviets did in fact exploit it to gain the upper hand, leaving the prospects for peace even more elusive. Then, in the early 80s, we shifted strategies and began dealing with the Soviets as global Level 3 masters who wanted to win. The "peace through strength" method was employed. The U.S. refused to play its designated role in the unreasonable person drama—subservience. We increased rather than decreased the strength of our military. For the Soviets, the expense of regaining and maintaining the superior position placed an unsustainable burden on their already faltering economy. Thus, military superiority, the master role, became economically impossible for them. This, plus the growing discontent of the masses within Russia and its satellite states, led to the downfall of the Soviet system and the end of the Cold War.

This is a story of good conflict with an unreasonable nation. The Cold War ended not because the U.S. was nice but because the U.S. was strong. It's not that the Soviets became reasonable, but that they became realistic. They changed because internal pressures made holding to their system no longer feasible. We didn't change their minds; we changed the conditions. And when the conditions changed, they changed their minds. Good conflict was achieved because the U.S. did two things: set relational boundaries and acknowledged relational realities.

Setting Relational Boundaries

With reasonable people we solve problems by working together to reach mutually satisfying solutions. Reasoning with reasonable people works, which makes for good conflict. But it doesn't work with unreasonable people because they don't have the necessary "reason muscles." And if we attempt it, the frustration we experience puts us right back into their drama.

Reasoning doesn't work, but a limited substitute does—setting boundaries. Boundaries accomplish what reasoning can't. He tried everything he could to convince the neighbor to leash the mutt but nothing worked. Finally he improved the situation by putting up a fence. In this case, the solution that couldn't be achieved through reasoning was achieved through boundaries. Yes, it cost him something, but it worked. With reasonable people, problems are solved when both sides participate in the reasoning process.

With unreasonable people, problems are "restrained" when the reasonable person does a good job of setting boundaries.

A gentle reminder: All aspects of dealing with unreasonable people—assessing them, avoiding their dramas, accepting the limits—are challenging. So challenging, in fact, that we won't succeed without the support of others. Unreasonable people can be so confounding, so determined, and so frustrating that we'll fail if we try to go it alone. The understanding and reinforcement of other reasonable people is not a luxury but a necessity. Slaves in the pre-Civil War South understood this well. For all practical purposes, their masters operated under this unreasonable set of assumptions: "We're good, you're bad, you exist for us. If you submit to our control, we'll get along just fine." Lack of submission led to physical harm. Their sufferings under that system of chattel slavery were eased somewhat by singing songs that came to be known as "Negro Spirituals." Through the lyrics, they expressed thoughts and feelings to each other about their trials, their tribulations, and their hopes. The ability to endure was enhanced through mutual encouragement.

We may not be literally enslaved by unreasonable people, but the need for support is just as essential. Remember, the unreasonable person believes his survival depends upon getting us to believe "There's nothing wrong with him, but there's definitely something wrong with us." Without reference points for our sanity that others provide, it's very easy to get swept into that distortion and become discouraged. **Good conflict with unreasonable people is achievable only with the support of reasonable people relationships.**

Let's look now at principles involved in setting relational boundaries with each of the three levels of unreasonable people.

Setting Boundaries with Level 1 (Dormant) Unreasonable People

Left to himself, the Level 1 unreasonable person doesn't change. But when the person he needs to entice into the drama refuses to cooperate, it creates conflict pressure. And if the pressure is high enough, he displays a surprising capacity to grow, which is why the word **dormant** is used. Our goal with a Level 1 unreasonable person is to use boundaries that promote **growth.** We can't make growth happen, but we can create conditions under which growth is more likely to occur. The experience of dealing with a Level 1 unreasonable person is very similar to that of being a toddler's parent, an elementary schoolteacher, or a coach. It takes a lot of work, but the outcome is worth the effort.

We have to be frustrating, persistent, and patient.

Be Frustrating

By advising you to be frustrating, I don't mean that we are to be maliciously hurtful. I do mean that we should intentionally frustrate the drama process by refusing to play our designated roles so the resulting discomfort gives the unreasonable person an incentive to grow. That's what happened in the grocery store checkout line when Penny refused to participate in the verbal tug of war with our daughter. When it became clear to our little girl that she couldn't get Penny to play her part, she was forced to grow up a little. Refusing roles such as subservience, gratefulness, rescuing, or pretending discombobulates the unreasonable person, making him feel uncomfortable. But that's good because that feeling may cause him or her to seek out more mature ways of relating.

Chapter 10: Dealing With Office Or Work Relationships

I just want to say a very quick word about office or work relationships as you may have to deal with them at some point in your management career. You may very well be the last to hear that two of your employees are in a relationship with one another but if you are very unlucky, you may have to deal with the fallout.

Many companies nowadays have policies surrounding employee relationships; they're often frowned upon, usually out of a desire to avoid accusations of sexual harassment or an unpleasant working environment should something go wrong.

There's nothing worse than a workplace couple that have split up who take out all their anger on each other – and nearby staff – at work. If the problems persist, you may have to look at moving one of the employees to a different work station, department or branch entirely.

As a general rule, however, as long as your company doesn't have a set policy about inter-office or inter-work dating, I'd be inclined to ignore it. That's assuming, of course, that the couple never bring their outside problems into the work environment. If it starts to become a problem, then a quick word with both and an informal warning will hopefully do the trick.

The exception here is you! If you as a manager are thinking of having a relationship with a member of your staff, think very carefully. You could be opening yourself and the company up to future claims of harassment should things not work out. Imagine the relationship ending badly and you both having to work together; you can't potentially solve the problem by moving the employee elsewhere as he or she could claim you are only doing it because of your personal history. Even if the relationship does work out, other members of staff could accuse you of favouritism. If you want to have a relationship with a subordinate, cover yourself by reporting it to your own boss and asking their advice.

Lazy Employees

Who they are: There are laid back employees and then there are just lazy employees; a laid back worker will do the work in their own relaxed way while a lazy worker will do everything they can to avoid the work in the first place. If you want a happy and productive workforce, you will have to take the latter to task. Lazy employees not only shirk responsibility – they might have to do some work otherwise – but they also lack initiative and get-up-and-go. Unless it's getting up and going for coffee, that is!

Lazy employees may very well spend an inordinate amount of time doing coffee runs, browsing the internet or taking extra time at lunch. They probably think that you won't notice. But of course, as they spend time away from the real tasks at hand, deadlines are being missed, money is being lost and other members of staff become resentful at having to cover for this lazy employee.

What to do:

Before you tackle it directly with the person concerned, collect your ammunition. Keep a precise track of their comings and goings; make a written note of how long they take for lunch and how many coffee breaks they have, and for how long. Keep a detailed record too of any work that is impacted negatively by the employee — is the fact that they are rarely at their desk or their post hindering someone else's role, for instance? Are any deadlines being missed or discreetly moved back? Keep a record of all and then consult with the employee.

Show them your notes and ask for clarification on the problems at hand; let them know up front that you have concerns about their performance and if they do not improve, they may well lose their job.

Be prepared to point out to them exactly how they should have done better so they cannot claim that they didn't know for the future.

Give the lazy worker a kick up the backside by setting specific goals and targets with deadlines that cannot be missed; follow up on every target. Warn them that their job may be at risk if they do not complete each task in the manner you have specified upfront. Encourage the employee to operate a priority task list and stick to it. Arrange a time to review the employee's subsequent performance.

If you see an improvement, praise them. The boost in morale might be just enough to see them continue to make an effort.

If they haven't improved, however, there may not be anything else for it but to terminate the lazy employee, always making sure that you follow the correct protocols and legal requirements, of course.

Let's visualise the opening to a dialogue between a manager and the lazy employee. In this case, the employee, Sarah, has already been spoken to several times about her behaviour. This is now make or break time for the employee's future in the company.

Chapter 11: How To Deal With A Difficult Boss And Still Keep Your Job

Some bosses are wonderful to work for. While they may expect you to work hard, they also make reasonable expectations and give you the freedom to find a balance between work and your personal life. Others, however, are overbearing, demanding and often set unrealistic expectations that can drive you crazy. If you work for a boss who falls into the latter group, you will need to find a way to deal with this boss in a respectful, reasonable way.

Effective Communication Skills

One of the best steps that you can take when working with a difficult boss is to utilize effective communication skills. If your boss is the type of person who likes to provide you with half-instructions or change instructions in the middle of a project, bring a notepad with you to each

meeting you have with them. Jot down any instructions they provides. Before you leave their presence, repeat the instructions that you have written down. This will accomplish two things. First, it provides your boss with the ability to add to the instructions before you begin working on the project. Second, it makes you look as though you are diligent and committed to following through on their instructions perfectly. It may be wise to follow up with your boss about the status of a project several times to ensure that your work meets their expectations.
Set Limits

It is important to understand your rights as a worker and to establish limits regarding your work hours and free time. Unless you have a position where you are required to be on-call, it is not reasonable or appropriate for your boss to call you during your off-hours regarding work-related manners. Let these calls go to voice mail. Listen to the messages, and send a quick text message to your boss saying that you are out-of-pocket. You will gladly talk to them about the issue bright and early on your next scheduled work day. Furthermore, avoid being roped into staying after hours if possible. Keep in mind that once you have established the precedence of staying late or working on the weekends, this may become an expectation.

Maintain Distance

It is important to maintain distance from your boss as much as possible. This is a person who you must work with and must take instructions from, but this does not mean that you need to hang out with the person all of the time. You can decrease your annoyance with this person and keep your blood pressure lower by working on your own as much as possible. Also, avoid extracurricular activities with your boss outside of the office. If you are permitted to, consider working from home as much as possible. Do what you need to do in order to keep your job and not appear to be standoffish. However, distance can be healthy when dealing with someone who irritates you.

Many people will deal with a difficult boss at one point or another. How you manage your relationship with this person will ultimately affect your sanity and your ability to keep your job. Follow these strategies to more effectively deal with your difficult boss.

Chapter 12: Getting Out Of Tight Situations

At times you have to get out of them for a while

Getting Out of Tight Situations

Some situations with difficult people tend to tighten too much. At

times you have to get out of them for a while to breathe in fresh

strength again, and later go back to the same situation to conquer it.

This kind of getting out is temporary, and is not meant to avoid

difficult people altogether.

Uniting with Others

You can join forces with your siblings to appease your difficult parents, or you may unite with other workers in pacifying a

difficult boss.

There's safety and strength in numbers.

You can encourage each other whenever the pressure gets too

strong.

You can help each other out in getting jobs done right.

Children can agree to lessen added hassles by avoiding friction

between themselves (They can appear to be more acceptable to their difficult parents).

If a solo performance of good attitude can do wonders to change

difficult people, then just imagine what a positive group of people can do?

A proverb says that two heads are better than one. It's not an alien

from another planet that's being portrayed here, but a unity in working out a positive course of action.

Joint acts of goodness are sure to overwhelm a single difficult

person.

Using Reverse Psychology

Most difficult people, being egoistic, are childish. Most tricks for spoiled kids are applicable to them. It pays to study how to pacify

tots in tantrums and apply that to difficult adults.

Reverse psychology is basically suggesting the positive opposite. It requires a touch of art to skillfully apply this.

Let's say a difficult person interferes while you're giving an

inspiring talk to a small group. He hints out that he knows better than you do.

So you stop and let the guy have his say.

Limit his time, then say something like: "That was interesting.

After I finish, I'm sure some of you here also want to say

something."

Stress the words "After I finish." This will give a hint to all,

especially to Mr. Difficult Guy, that you don't want any interruption until you are done talking.

The famous sermon on the mount, given by Jesus, taught that it pays to always do more than is being asked by difficult people.

If they ask you to carry a bag in one mile, carry it two miles.

If they ask for your cloak, give them your other garments as well. If they slap you on the right cheek, offer the other as well.

In this way, the sermon tells us you "heap up burning coals in their

heads."

This means you make them re-think their behavior compared to

yours.

The re-thinking can only happen if those difficult people see

something different and positive in you.

If you confront them head-on, then you have just proven yourself to be another difficult person.

Think of an animal trainer. Animal trainers always have food at

hand to reward performing animals.

Some use whips and other tools, like the lion or tiger trainers.

But some teach animals by giving them a dose of their own

medicine. They let the animals do foolish things. When the animals get hurt by doing such acts, they learn never to do them again.

Of course, never treat difficult people like animals.

But you can handle them by hinting at their foibles, by letting them

suffer or see the consequences of such, and by giving them a dose of their own medicine.

Using Humor

Long time ago, colonized people used comedy plays to protest the

cruelty of their colonizers in a light way. They communicated the

message to both countrymen and oppressors effectively by making fun of everyday scenes of injustices.

Humor can drive the point home without directly condemning the

offenders. It can make both the offending and offended parties laugh and yet learn.

In one Christmas party I attended, the employees thought of

presenting a comedy skit where both employees and employers were impersonated in a comical way.

They all saw themselves in a new light.

They realized their strengths and weaknesses, as well as what

images they have been projecting to others.

If difficult people try to make everyone see how ugly you are, you

may start calling them Mr. Handsome or Miss Beautiful, not with a look of insult but with sincerity.

Mean it.

It will either make them feel ashamed of themselves, so they will

stop; or they will feel accomplished, so they will mellow down because they think they have proven their point.

Relaxation

When under attack, relax. You can't die of severe attacks from difficult people unless you choose to.

If you think too highly of yourself (that's feeding the ego), chances

are you will easily be offended by difficult people.

On the other hand, if you estimate yourself just right, and you don't

pay attention to what difficult people think about you (because you

know better than to take their remarks seriously), no damage will be done no matter how severe the attacks.

You can just smile away at the offenders.

Relaxing is one of the greater virtues not even the most extremely

wealthy people possess.

For sure, difficult people can never relax because they don't know

how. They actually hate the idea. Relaxation to them is mortal sin.

Thus, they also deprive people around them of rest and relaxation.

They need to see that everybody is pressured.

But once they see that you can relax under attack, they will begin

to avoid you.

They may spread the news around that you are lazy and won't

amount to anything.

To them, tension leads to sure success.

Not only can you save yourself from difficult people by relaxing,

you can also maintain good health.

Practice relaxing in any situation: While reading, eating,

conversing, sitting or standing, walking, catching a bus, being scolded, in an emergency, etc.

It will be difficult at first; but as you practice, it will become

spontaneous.

The body can be taught and conditioned by the mind.

Don't surrender your fate to circumstances around you.

Take control. Never control others (that's being a difficult person),

but learn to control yourself.

Many say it is important to let your temper show, because

repressed emotions are bad for the heart.

Relaxing is not repressing anything in you.

Uncontrolled tempers only make matters worse.

There is a saying that a fool gives full bent to his emotions, but the

wise refrains from them.

So at the first sign of a threat from difficult people, relax. Don't let

their wishes dictate how you live your life.

Showing Them

There will be times when difficult people become too intolerable, especially when other people are greatly affected.

During these rare times, you must speak out and rebuke the

offenders gently.

There was once a difficult young man who was giving an old lady a hard time on a train. A young lady stood up and asked him to be patient with the old woman then invited him to join her in giving the old woman a hand.

When I was in a conference once, a difficult person stood up to ask

lots of questions that led nowhere.

The speaker gently cut him short and then said, "I will answer one

question, sir, but the rest of your questions will be dealt with after

my speech so we will not run out of time."

Sometimes, difficult people must be shown that they have gone

beyond their limits. But this must be done gently and free from any harmful intention, especially from public humiliation.

We don't want to merely stop difficult people; we also want to help

them.

Shifting Attention

When difficult people start hammering away at you, try to divert your attention to positive things.

If a difficult spouse is consistently nagging about your son's failing

grades in math or science, shift your spouse's attention to subjects where your son got better grades.

Learn to take attention away from an unwanted subject matter. Consider this story.

John, a difficult person, was jealous of Jack because Jill (John's

crush) was closer to Jack.

So John ridiculed Jack's face to everybody in a party, and made

sure Jill took special notice.

Jill tried to save Jack's face by suddenly asking everyone if they

have heard the latest news on avian flu.

Jack took the cue and began discussing the disease and the whole

group was instantly converted to their side. John, wanting to be the

star of the show, put himself forward and tried to dominate the discussion.

Jack and Jill settled back, contented to be part of John's audience.

It's better to be John's audience than to be his victim.

Another technique of shifting attention is to pass the pressure on to others.

This is very effective in a public speaking situation. You may find

this handy in a small group discussion where you act as a speaker or lecturer.

If a difficult person is asking you senseless (those that have no

connection whatsoever to the topic) questions, or if that individual

just wants to interfere with the discussion, you may either:

1. Entertain questions later (which is a temporary

diversionary technique); or

2. Deal with the question now by throwing the same

question to the group.

For instance, Mr. X asks a series of questions on abortion. Your topic is human anatomy.

Abortion can be connected to the human anatomy, but it is likely

that majority of your audience did not come to hear you speak on abortion.

But Mr. X keeps on pressing his questions, trying to put you in a

bad light.

One of his questions is: "What if, after aborting the baby, guilt

strikes you and you decide to put the fetus back? How do you do

it?"

You say to the audience, "Listen up, guys. Mr. X here has an

interesting question. He wants to know how a fetus could be put back into the womb. Who can answer this?"

By doing the above, you get the pressure off you and you put it

back to Mr. X.

Now, the whole audience is after him.

For sure, people who came there to hear about the human anatomy

will be irked. They will answer as meanly as Mr. X asked the question.

Here's another story.

A difficult man wanted to change the route when he and his friends

went on a trip to the wilds.

The difficult guy desperately wanted to try a new path and

doggedly pressured the leader of the tour to do this.

The leader knew that the rest of the group, and especially the

owner and driver of the car, preferred the usual route and showed signs of impatience on the difficult guy's insistence.

The leader spoke up: "I really have no problem with your request,

as long as the driver and owner of the car has no problem with it."

By doing so, the leader just saved himself from the pressure and

the majority resentment had he succumbed to the difficult guy's demands.

Majority Approval

Mr. Manager is faced with a difficult employee who insists on

introducing a union which he knows is abhorred by the majority of the employees.

He does not want to sound anti-unionism, so what he does is call a

meeting of all the employees and submit the matter to a "yes or no" vote.

As expected, the "no" votes have it.

He then had the department supervisors and department heads sign

the resolution; thus making it appear that it was not he who turned down the request for a union but the employees themselves.

Putting It In Black and White

When dealing with difficult people, especially in sensitive matters

like favors, money, or appointments, it will help you to put

everything in writing.

Companies make policies precisely for dealing with difficult

employees.

When difficult friends or relatives borrow a big sum of money

from you, have them sign an agreement to pay the price on a definite date.

This is ideal for those who have a track record of unpaid debts.

If an appointment for a meeting is set with difficult people, keep

repeating to them the details. If possible, let them text to your cell

phone the time and place so you may have a record of your appointment that they themselves have set up.

If difficult employees insist on something unreasonable, it is safe to make policies or regulations regarding employee rights, duties, and privileges which employees have to sign as part of their work contract.

You can go back to the provisions of these policies or regulations

as you deal with them in the future.

Difficult people are so finicky about whatever details they can use

to annoy people and to prove to them that they have erred.

Difficult people enjoy it when they catch a person unprepared and

at a loss.

Thus, you may have to deal with them according to their ways. A

proverb says: "At times we must deal with fools according to their foolishness; though at times, we must also deal with them

differently."

Going Against the Flow

There are times you must remain meek and silent as you deal with difficult people.

There are times you must go with their line of thinking for a while

to ease their pressures.

But there are times you have to shut them up without losing your

dignity.

But then there are times you have to simply do the opposite of

what they want you to do.

If they make fun of you, you simply look at them and ask, "So I

look stupid. What's so funny about that?"

In doing this, make sure there are no other people around, or these

difficult people may get what they want, and everybody may end

up laughing at you. If this happens, laugh with them. This will neutralize the situation.

At times you have to shut your mouth if these difficult people goad

you to speak. Or speak when they want you to shut your mouth.

But do this without any ill feelings against the offenders. Just teach them a lesson.

It must be stressed that this strategy is not always advisable. You

must be keenly sensitive to situations before you can masterfully apply this technique.

Applicability of techniques is on a case-to-case basis.

Hence, dealing with difficult people takes lots of practice to master.

Don't be afraid to commit mistakes. Mistakes, when taken with

maturity, will make us wiser. The wiser we get, the more we master, and the more we can help.

Leaving the "Show"

When things really get out of hand and every option has become useless, the best thing to do to be free from a tight situation is to

excuse yourself from the scene politely.

Just leave.

There's no use spending your energy in fighting a dragon like Don

Quixote.

But make sure you excuse yourself gracefully so as not to lose

face. Smile. Chin up. Make sure your last note is a friendly one.

Of course, difficult people will think that they have won that

round. But that's the way they always think. You can never make them think otherwise. So why fuss? Let them think all they want. What matters most is that you attain peace and solitude.

Conclusion

Difficult people of all kinds are inevitable in life. You will run into people who behave in ways that do not align with your intents and goals. These people seem determined to make your life harder, but in reality, their behavior is probably not aimed directly at you. You can make the best of these situations and actually get along better with difficult people.

It is important to understand that all people are different. What you want is probably never going to match what someone else wants. Misaligned goals and other differences often lead to the conflict that makes human interaction difficult. Overcoming differences requires patience and good communication.

Sometimes, people act difficult for reasons that have nothing to do with you. You need to stop taking the difficult behavior of others so personally. Try to be more empathetic and improve communication. Approach difficult people as a challenge to be overcome. Find the source of their difficult behavior, and work with people to find an ideal solution for it.

Other times, people act difficult because they are envious of you or angry with you. Handling the emotions of other people that are directed at you can be nerve-wracking. You may have to swallow your pride and apologize to someone for a transgression. Alternatively, you can just walk away and not deal with the drama at all.

Loved ones are often the most difficult people of all. Handling fights, deception, manipulation, and other issues with loved ones can be very hard. It can also be very hurtful. You must remember to remain caring and loving with your loved ones as you try to find out why they are being so difficult. Work with them to help heal the behavior, rather than fight with them.

You really can safely and gently deal with difficult people while avoiding drama and fights. There are ways to maturely address the issues you have with others without leading to further conflict. You will be surprised how well people respond to you if you make an effort to reach an agreeable solution with them.

However, sometimes you just have to walk away from some people. You cannot reasonably tolerate people who are more difficult to deal with than they are worth. You have the right to avoid unhappiness and drama in your life, but some people just bring emotional turmoil and conflict along with them wherever they go. You must clear useless baggage from your life and surround yourself with enjoyable, positive people. Some people offer no value to your life, so cut them off.

You cannot change difficult people. But you can change yourself. Changing your attitude and your reactions toward difficult people can drastically change your interpersonal interactions. You may suddenly find yourself encountering fewer difficult interactions and fewer difficult people as you become more understanding and more communicative.

Using the tips in this book can help you unlock a new level of peace and ease in your life as you end difficult conflicts with other people. You can use the tips contained in these pages to learn how to deal with different types of difficult people in more effective manners. You can also use this book as a guide on how to achieve better communication and conflict resolution skills. From walking away to becoming a better communicator, this book has all sorts of advice that you need to start solving the problems that you run into with more difficult people.

Your life will be much easier if you learn to stop inadvertently causing conflict and judging people. You will feel better if you stop taking difficult behavior personally. You can smooth out the bumps in your life significantly just by changing your own behavior. You cannot reasonably change others, and if you try, you will be frustrated and disappointed. But if you change your own behavior, you will find that others will respond to you differently. You can influence them to behave differently. You hold the power to turn difficult people and situations around fast, and this book will help you unlock that power.

Thanks for reading!

www.ingramcontent.com/pod-product-compliance
Lightning Source LLC
Chambersburg PA
CBHW071452070526
44578CB00001B/313